A L

HIS

OF

ENGLAND

David Ross

Illustrations by John Short

APPLETREE PRESS

First published in 1997 by
The Appletree Press Ltd,
19 -21 Alfred Street, Belfast BT2 8DL
Tel. +44 (0) 1232 243074
Fax. +44 (0) 1232 246756
Copyright © 1997 The Appletree Press Ltd.
Printed in the U.A.E. All rights reserved.
No part of this publication may be
reproduced or transmitted in any form
or by any means, electronic or mechanical,
photocopying, recording or any information
and retrieval system, without permission
in writing from the publisher.

A Little History of England

A catalogue record for this book is
available from the British Library

ISBN 0-86281-569-X

9 8 7 6 5 4 3 2 1

Contents

"In England there are sixty different religions, and only one sauce."

- Francesco Carracioli

"The English have all the materials required for a revolution. What they lack is the spirit of generalisation and revolutionary ardour."

- *Karl Marx*

INTRODUCTION

The history of England is a very large subject for a small book. This little book, however, does not aim to cover every twist and turn of politics and warfare or describe the reign of every king or queen. Sheep and Shakespeare, Cromwell and coal, Romans and Romantics, and many other elements make up the fabric of English history. Those elements are used to light up the main themes, showing how the nation grew, and how England came to play its crucial part in the shaping of the modern world.

Hadrian's Wall

THE PEOPLES OF ENGLAND, AND THEIR LANGUAGE

England occupies two-thirds of a large island, detached from Europe only some twelve thousand years ago. Half the size of France, it has still been large enough in resources and population to be one of the great powers of Western Europe. It has been inhabited by humans since the Stone Age. Long before recorded history, its empty forests and green hills attracted incomers. We know them only by the artifacts they have left, their burial grounds, and a few spectacular sites which have survived, like Stonehenge. What language they spoke is unknown.

In the centuries before Christ, the land was overrun by Celtic tribes who had migrated from east and north of the Mediterranean Sea, their iron weapons helping them to force back, wipe out or enslave the Bronze Age inhabitants. After Julius Caesar's brief expedition of 55 BC, the Romans came in force in the first century AD, and the history of England began to be recorded. The Romans called the country Britannia, after the name of a Celtic tribe, the Brythones. For three hundred out of England's two thousand years of recorded history, it was a Roman colony. A small number of high-ranking Romans, and some ten thousand legionaries, many of them from other Roman colonies like Pannonia (now Slovenia), imposed order on the tribesmen.

As the Roman empire collapsed in the fifth century, the vigorous tribes from across the North Sea and the Channel came roaring in: Angles and Saxons. It was the Celts' turn to retreat to the ancient hill-forts and the rugged extremities of the country.

But certain basic things had been established - routes, river and hill-names, holy sites. The Roman roads dictated transport and settlement patterns long after their careful paving was lost in muddy ruts; the speakers of Germanic languages still used the Celtic names for rivers like the Avon. Roman forts (castra) are preserved in the names of Chester, Doncaster and many other places.

Between the fifth and the tenth centuries, the concept of England replaced that of Britannia. The Roman provinces had vanished. They were replaced by a collection of Anglo-Saxon petty kingdoms, their frontiers uncertain, each struggling to survive and dominate. Then, in the eighth century and onwards, from the sea to west and east, the Norsemen struck. Originally from Denmark and Norway, their fleets had established bases in Ireland and Orkney. In the space of a couple of generations they established control over a huge part of eastern England. Following the long-established pattern, they came as raiders and ended as settlers.

In this era of constant, sporadic warfare between tribal groups, a drift towards centralised power can hardly have been noticed. Yet, through the generations, it was happening, aided by two things: one was the Church, which established its own frail but effective network across the tribal boundaries; the other was the language. The new settlers, Norsemen apart, spoke essentially the same language: cousin to Dutch and German. They spoke it with a variety of different accents and many regional variations. But Old

Section of the Bayeaux Tapestry

The Tower of London is an early Norman keep

English became a written language early on, partly because Latin, except as a religious language, had died out with the departure of the Romans. The laws of the kings, and the poems of their bards were written in Old English. From an early stage, their language helped to give the immigrants the sense of being a single people: the English.

By the eleventh century, England's boundaries had virtually taken the shape they have today. To the West was Wales, a Celtic land protected by its mountains and speaking a Celtic language. To the North was Scotland, also emerging as a separate kingdom.

The final conquest came in 1066, with the invasion of the Normans under William, Duke of Normandy. Like the Romans nine hundred years before, the Normans were few in number but they won mastery over the population. Whilst the Romans did it through the power and mobility of their armies, the Normans did it by spreading thinly across the country, each knight or baron speedily building a castle, perhaps only of wood to start with, later replaced by stone, from which he could dominate his allotted tract of land.

They held the ground by right of conquest, they depended on one another's aid if the natives rebelled, and their right of tenure could be guaranteed only by the king. From William I onwards, the power of the King, ruling from his new fortress in London, was great. How great, and how effectively it was deployed, depended on the monarch's own ability and strength of character, and on that of his chief servants.

The Normans spoke an early form of French, and this became the language of the court and officialdom. For two hundred years, English, ignored by the ruling class and scholars in favour of Latin and French, developed as the language of the people. In daily use it was slowly changing, becoming simpler in its grammar, and absorbing many new words. Had the Normans been more numerous, English might have been stifled, and a form of French would have replaced it. But the Normans, especially those living away from London, gradually came to see England as their homeland, and they began to speak the language of the majority of the population. By the 13th century, English was not just the speech of the Saxon peasant, and by the mid-14th century, when Chaucer wrote The Canterbury Tales, it was once again the language of politics, of learning, and of culture. French survived only in the law-courts.

The floods of human invasion into England had ceased with the Scandinavians. But throughout the centuries, there were trickles of incomers. Jewish communities were established in larger towns from the 10th century. In the 16th century, after the Reformation, many French Protestants (Huguenots) settled in England, as did refugees from Flanders, where in the 17th century a bloody war of independence was fought against the Spanish empire. In the 18th century there was a substantial black population, of slaves and servants, especially in Bristol and London, which was to disappear, absorbed into the genetic stream. In the early-19th century many Irish immigrants came, driven by the Famine or lured by the expanding industrial economy; in the later part there were many from Baltic Europe and Russia, especially Jews fleeing persecution. In the middle of the 20th century came the immigrants from the rapidly-dissolving Empire. England's larger cities and towns became multi-racial communities, importing traditions and beliefs that were new to England but often older than England. From this ancient and modern mixture the English are still emerging, the same yet

English Bowmen at Crecy (1346)

American War of Independence

different.

Forgetting the other countries within the mini-continent of Britain, the English have often thought of their own country as an island. And in terms of mainland Europe, of course it has been. But islands are open and exposed places, expected to take in those wrecked by storms elsewhere. At different times, England has been hospitable and inhospitable to incomers, reflecting the nation's own confidence and security, or lack of them. In the 13th century, the government expelled the Jews. In the later 20th, successive governments have made entry steadily more difficult.

The English language, always an easy one to make new words in, acquired a vast range of rude terms to describe foreigners. Chief victims were the French, who enthusiastically returned the insults. "To run off like an Englishman" is what the French say; the English phrase is "to take French leave." The French were the nearest foreigners, they were richer, and more numerous. The English kings' long struggle to hold or extend their French lands meant that for seven centuries the English were to regard the French primarily as enemies. Great victories over France like Crecy (1346) or Agincourt (1415) were long remembered, the fact that England was gradually ousted from France was overlooked. Yet throughout the same period, because of France's supply of luxury goods, especially wine, and because of her lead over England in cultural matters (much of the new arts of the Renaissance, in the 15th and 16th centuries, were passed on to England through France) there was a continuous French influence on many aspects of English life.

It was especially strong in military affairs, architecture, costume, and social correctness. Cross-Channel rivalries continued through the 18th-century empire-building period in North America, and culminated in the wars following the French revolutions and the rise of Napoleon. After the unification of Germany in 1870 and its emergence as a major power, it was quite a shock to the English to perceive the French as their chief ally.

Relations with other countries were less firmly set in traditional attitudes. Until 1534 England, as a Catholic country, had had close ties with the Papacy in Rome. All European states had their quarrels with the Pope, and England was no exception. These disputes were partly financial - government objections to the wealth of the Church - and partly political because of the Pope's spiritual authority. It was the Pope's refusal to grant Henry VIII a divorce from his first wife Katharine of Aragon that led to the break.

Before that, England had often seemed to be one of the most solidly-Catholic nations. English crusaders had fought in the Holy Land, and later helped to drive the Islamic Moors from Spain. Spain's king married the Catholic Queen Mary Tudor in 1554, but his country became the prime enemy during the reign of her sister Elizabeth I, when Spain's empire overseas was vast and England's scarcely beginning. Holland was sometimes an ally and trading partner, sometimes - as her power at sea and her Eastern empire grew - an enemy. Unconquered England got a nasty fright in 1667 when a hostile Dutch fleet came right up the Medway estuary in Kent.

England's empire spread the English, and their language, around the globe. There was great enterprise and purpose among the 16th-century merchant adventurers and the explorers, geographers, treasure-seekers and religious dissidents who followed them across the Atlantic, or round the Cape of Good Hope and eventually on to the Antipodes. (Only the criminals, "transported" to the new

colonies, had no choice in the matter.) They sought profit, knowledge or security, and out of their efforts and commercial rivalries with the French and Dutch, the empire took shape. But there was no consistent drive and purpose behind it.

The American colonies' rebellion took the government by surprise. These English communities chose to become foreigners. Their successful war of independence was a blow to the nation's prestige, but the Royal Navy's successes at sea and the later victories over the French restored it. Relations with the United States continued to be somewhat touchy on both sides through the 19th century, despite close trade and cultural exchange. In India, during the 18th and 19th centuries, a few thousand soldiers, administrators and traders arranged the affairs of a vast empire just as Normans and Romans had done to their remote ancestors.

Statue of King Alfred, Winchester

THE UNEASY GLORY OF THE KINGS

From the days of the Angles and Saxons, the English have been accustomed to rule by a monarch, and a hereditary royal family. The early kings, or tribal chiefs, were war-leaders and settlers of disputes. From this latter role came their position as law-givers. The basic laws, relating to property-owning, theft and killing, were written down in Old English. At first this was to help the king to deal fairly with his people, but it also meant that, having made the law, he had to follow it. Already the law was something beyond the king's whim. The king also held periodic assemblies at which his retainers and subsidiary nobles would gather. Half-feast, half council, they asserted the king's authority but also enabled the affairs of the kingdom to be openly discussed. Among the most important members of such gatherings were the clergy.

Britannia had been Christian. The Germanic and Nordic invaders and settlers who made England were pagans. In 597 AD a Roman bishop, Augustine, was sent by the Pope to begin the missionary process. His base was Canterbury in Kent which remains the religious capital of England. Kent was a separate kingdom then. The strategy of the Christian missionaries was to convert the king and his family. Once this was achieved, and permission given to establish churches throughout the kingdom, it was possible through a mixture of persuasion, teaching and compulsion to baptise the

Colman of Lindisfarne

population, though several generations would pass before Christianity became grounded in the minds of the people.

From the north and west, the Celtic Christians also sent missionaries. Their practices were not entirely the same as those of the men from Rome and once a network of bishoprics covered the country, tensions emerged between the two sources. Although the ostensible debate was on such matters as the dating of Easter, the true conflict related to how the Church should be organised and governed. At the Synod of Whitby in 664, the Roman churchmen won, and England became a Roman Catholic country, its Church answerable to the Pope in Rome.

The boundaries of the first bishoprics corresponded broadly to those of the kingdoms of the time. The bishop, because of his status as God's representative, his learning and his power as the man in charge of the Church's increasing wealth, soon became a key figure in the king's council. Church and government were separate, but closely linked. Some of the Anglo-Saxon kings abdicated to become monks. Most made pilgrimages to Rome. The second-last Anglo-Saxon king, Edward the Confessor, was exceptionally pious, and such kings were generous to the Church. Huge areas of the country came to be owned by abbeys, and abbots and bishops inevitably became important figures in public life.

At one time, in the ninth century, it looked as though the Danes might conquer all of England. But a Saxon revival began under Alfred the Great, king of Wessex, whose fight back made him the first English folk-hero and established a pattern. Bouncing back from apparent defeat became an English speciality, right up to World War II, and the retreat from Dunkirk in 1940. A descendant of Alfred's, Athelstan, became the first king of a unified England in 926, accepted as overlord by any remaining regional "kings". Even after that, Scandinavians occasionally took over the throne, notably Cnut, famous for showing his flatterers the limitations of kingship by his failure to turn back the rising tide. But even under a Danish king, England was recognised as a separate nation, and not integrated into a Scandinavian empire.

Under the Normans and their successors, the power of the king was greatly increased, and so was the power of his great servants. Rifts began to open between Church and State, as the leaders of the Church were torn between their spiritual allegiance to the Pope, their responsibility to the Church, and the demands of the kings, who resented the Pope's ability to interfere and were increasingly jealous of the Church's wealth. This came to a head with the murder of the Archbishop of Canterbury, Thomas Becket, in his cathedral, in 1170, at the order of king Henry II. Four years later Henry humbly apologised, on the very spot where Beckett was slain. In the centuries to come, other bishops would be assassinated or executed, but it would be for their actions as servants of the king, not of the Pope.

From 1066 until 1558, the English monarch also ruled possessions in France. At different times these varied from Normandy, to almost all of France in the early 15th century under Henry V, to the single town of Calais, finally ceded to the French in 1558. Some English kings spent more time in their French lands than in England. The Hundred Years' War, fought on French soil intermittently through the 14th and 15th centuries, reflected the claims and counter-claims of successive members of the House of Plantagenet and others for the rich duchies of France. At length, despite defeats and disasters, the beleaguered French monarchy slowly and painfully extended its rule over all of France, and forced the English back to their own shoreline.

Kingship was the basis of society. The monarch was at the very top of the social order, and the source of law and government. A weak king, like Stephen in the 12th century, could result in the country falling into chaos. A strong king, like Edward I, could turn the state into something not unlike a military dictatorship. An incompetent king like his son, Edward II, could be murdered. But no king could rule without the support of his chief barons. King John discovered this in 1215, when his barons compelled him to sign the document called Magna Carta, which spelled out their rights and liberties, and thus the limitations of his own power. The Crown owned great estates, but never enough to pay for all the king might want to do.

Shrine of Thomas Beckett, Canterbury Cathedral

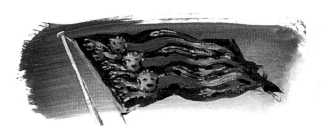

More money was always needed, particularly to pay the costs of making war. Except for fighting the Scots, the English always needed ships as well as the other elements of an army, and this was a heavy additional expense. Fines and customs duties were a prime source of income, but sometimes it was necessary to impose taxes, always a tricky business with the English. Public riots achieved the abolition of a poll-tax on individuals in the 14th century and again in the 1990s.

Parliament began not as an instrument of the people but as an instrument of the king. It was the royal court of Parliament, and it was summoned by the king to ensure that his policies were promoted throughout the land by those best equipped to do it - the lords and bishops. But it also provided a means of responding to the king if his policy was disputed in the country. Even the autocratic Edward I called frequent Parliaments, not to raise the taxes he needed, but to help in gathering them. Since before the Norman Conquest England had been organised into shires, each under the authority of the sheriff, who was the king's representative, and boroughs: the larger towns with their own administration. At times of dispute between king and barons, each found it useful to draw in representatives of shire and town, to gain their support. By 1341, the structure had developed into a House of Commons and a House of Lords, with of course the latter having far more prestige and power. By the 1350s, though Parliament was making laws, it was at the king's behest. It was still summoned by the king and dismissed by him, as he pleased. The king still ruled, through his Privy Council.

Oliver Cromwell

PARLIAMENT'S RISE TO SUPREMACY

In the late fifteenth century, the focus of armed struggle moved away from France to an internal dispute, the Wars of the Roses. The complicated genealogy of royalty had resulted in two related family groups, based on the neighbouring duchies of York and Lancaster, claiming the right to the kingship. It was a dynastic political struggle rather than a great military upheaval. As in a murderous dance, Yorkist king overthrew Lancastrian king, to be overthrown in turn. Richard III had his nephews, the boy-king Edward V and his brother, strangled. The Battle of Bosworth (1485) resolved matters with the throne being taken by Henry Tudor. Even then, pretenders like Perkin Warbeck (executed 1496) turned up, claiming to be the true heir to the throne. (The Tudors, incidentally, were of Welsh descent, the Stuarts who followed them were Scottish; they were followed by Germans. Royal families intermarried frequently and knew no boundaries.)

By the beginning of the 16th century, the Church in England was in a bad way. The demand for reform begun by Martin Luther in Germany soon spread to England, where there had been a tradition of dissent - the Lollards - going back more than a hundred years. The Church was rich, comfortable, somewhat corrupt, and lazy. Not for religious reasons but for dynastic and financial reasons, the second Tudor king, Henry VIII, with his minister Thomas Cromwell in the space of a few years abolished the thousands of monasteries took their wealth, and sold off their lands. It was a revolutionary act, but the Church, of which Henry made himself - and hi successors - Supreme Head, was powerless. The days of archbishop as Chancellors of England were over. Thomas Cromwell was trained as a lawyer. Religion could still rouse fierce passions, and ever warfare, but the Church was now a department of state and not a separate power in the land.

Wealth and industry grew strongly through the sixteenth century and Parliament's importance grew too, though in the reigns o Elizabeth I and her successor James I, the royal Council decided matters. When the fanatical Catholics of the "Gunpowder Plot' tried to blow up Parliament in 1605, it was because the king and hi councillors, the real targets, would be there. But Parliament had grown strong enough by the 1640s to challenge the king. Charles was a stubborn autocrat, who sought to raise taxes without calling a Parliament. Many people were fiercely anti-Catholic; many remained secret Catholics too, and Charles was suspected o wanting to restore the Roman Church. The Parliamentary party with a strong Puritan element, had a mixture of economic and religious motives. Charles, king of both Scotland and England managed to provoke a Scottish invasion of England. In the end, ir 1642, civil war broke out. At first, the Royalists seemed to have the upper hand. But the Parliamentarians, who always held London reorganised their army into a highly efficient fighting-machine. Ir 1649 Charles I was beheaded in London, not the first king to be killed but the first to be tried by a court and condemned. England was governed by a Lord Protector, Oliver Cromwell.

The experiment did not last after Cromwell's death. Charles II was recalled from exile in Holland in 1660, and the monarchy was restored. Most people were relieved. Charles's successor, James II, was however openly Catholic, and found that this would not be tolerated. It was not Parliament that forced him out, but a self-appointed group of notables, who appealed to the Dutch prince William of Orange to come and claim the throne. William and his wife Mary (James's daughter) became joint sovereigns in the "Glorious Revolution" of 1688. The heirs of James II lived on abroad, as "Pretenders" to the throne. Legally, their claim was just, but the English nation, caught between traditional loyalty to the true king, and their fear of a religion they had been taught to distrust, rejected the Catholic Stuarts. When Queen Anne died in 1714, having outlived all seventeen of her children, the men of power looked abroad again, and found a suitable prince with a drop of Stuart blood in his heredity. George, Elector of Hanover, added the realm of England to his modest German possessions.

Two pro-Stuart rebellions in Scotland did nothing to endear the exiled line to the English, and the year of 1745 saw panic in London when a Highland army under Prince Charles Edward Stuart got

Elizabeth I

within a hundred miles of the capital before turning back. England was, on the whole, content to accept the Protestant Hanoverians on the throne.

William III had acceded very much on Parliament's terms, though even then, the king's Privy Council remained the real government. But royal power gradually diminished. The basis of modern Parliament emerged in the 18th century, with two opposing political parties. Whigs, usually with a more reformist outlook, and Tories, usually more concerned to preserve things as they had been, came in and out of government, voted in by a tiny electorate of property-owners, and given power at the behest of the king.

Step by step the framework of a constitutional monarchy grew. A series of reforms from 1832 made Parliament more representative of the people as a whole. (It was 1928 before women received the vote on the same basis as men.) Kings in the 18th century still pulled the strings of government. In the 19th century, though her ministers gave Queen Victoria the title of Empress of India, it was the Prime Minister and his Cabinet who decided the policy of the state, not the Queen and her Council.

Today the monarch still opens Parliament, and signs its Acts, which only become law on signature. The functions are ceremonial, and the House of Commons is supreme. The House of Lords (still unelected) lost its veto in 1911, not without a controversy. But the tradition of the monarchy goes back a long way. It survived disastrous kings like Edward II, mad ones like Henry VI or George III. As an institution it has shown great resilience, though it is now far more at the mercy of public opinion than ever before.

ENGLISH SOCIETY:
THIS HAPPY BREED OF MEN

"This royal throne of kings, this sceptred isle...
This fortress built by nature for herself
Against infection and the hand of war,
This happy breed of men, this little world,
This precious stone set in the silver sea,
Which serves it in the office of a wall
Or as a moat defensive to a house,
Against the envy of less happier lands,
This blessed plot, this earth, this realm, this England."
   - King Richard II, William Shakespeare

"The rich man in his castle,
The poor man at his gate,
God made them, high and lowly,
And ordered their estate."
   - All Things Bright and Beautiful, 19th century hymn

Apart from the fact that one is poetry and the other merely rhyme, these two extracts reveal something of the notions of the English about themselves at different times. In the 19th century they knew themselves to be the world's super-power, thanks to the wide spread empire and the equally wide spread Royal Navy. But there were deep divisions in society. In the 16th century, when Shakespeare wrote, England felt much more like a close-knit little island-state, struggling against her more powerful neighbours on the mainland of Europe (as again in 1940).

The islander mentality encourages an aloofness, a distinct standpoint, a sense that here things are done differently. This can lead to a sense of despondency as well as to a sense of superiority, but on the whole, throughout their history the English appear to have been well-satisfied with their station in the world. Large enough to be in Europe's big league, small enough to feel a sense of national identity that has for centuries overlain regional loyalties, well provided with wood, water, coal, and fertile ground, and with a temperate climate, they benefited from natural advantages.

Just as the isolation of Australia meant that its animals evolved in a separate way, so England's relative isolation has meant a degree of separate evolution. English history is part of the history of Western Europe. The institutions of the state developed in the same way and at much the same times as those of France, Spain and other countries. The same process took them all from tribalism to a centrally-managed state. But in England, more so than elsewhere, things were not done proscriptively. Most notably the law was based on traditional practice and previous decisions, not on the Roman code used in other countries. There was an acceptance of a shared set of aspirations, a common understanding of how things are done. It was assumed that the nation would pull together when necessary, in time of war for example, and otherwise get on with its own business. For centuries, local government through the country was left to the gentry. The English boarding school was a model of the system, where the masters let the boys run the place to a remarkable degree, relying on entrenched tradition and practice to prevent

Eton Schoolboys

anarchy. The system's defects are all too well-known, but it certainly worked. In the same way, certain professions, including medicine and the law, are still self-governing today.

The early establishment of law and kingship in England helped to promote the sense of freedom under authority. People could be relied on not to go to an extreme. The debit side is that into the English psyche crept a sort of laziness, a feeling that to be seen to try too hard was bad form. The story of Sir Francis Drake, finishing his game of bowls before setting sail to defeat the Spanish Armada in 1588, is emblematic of that. The gifted amateur who wins against the highly-trained professional had and still has a lot of appeal to the English mind.

Another aspect of that mind-set is a distrust of theories and systems. The English gazed with a mixture of admiration and horror at the French Revolution and the wholesale changes that followed, to administration, the calendar, the measurements, to say nothing of the massacres. A whole society was being turned upside down. Many people in England desired reform, but very few would have gone so far. Even at the height of public unrest and official panic during the slump after the Napoleonic Wars, there was no national upheaval. The worst event was the "Peterloo" Massacre in Manchester, which resulted in the deaths of eleven demonstrators. There was great tolerance in the national spirit. Pragmatism - a focus on the practical details of life, rather than on high ideals - has been seen as the English virtue. The same pragmatism, of course, gives rise to the French criticism of "perfidious Albion," a country with no principles except that of maintaining its own interest at all costs.

But England is too large for generalisations to be safe. While it may be true to say that in England revolutionaries knock on the door rather than jump in through the window, there have always been people prepared to stand against the order of things, however great the odds. For religion, like the Catholic Edmund Campion, hanged in 1581. For political principle, like the parliamentarian John Hampden, killed in action in 1643. For civil rights, like Wat Tyler, leader of the Peasants' Revolt, beheaded in 1381. For humanity, like William Wilberforce, campaigner against slavery at the end of the 18th century. For science, like Darwin setting out his theory of evolution against a howl of outrage. There have always been differing points of view. The severe, uncompromising Puritan ethic adopted by many people during the 16th and 17th centuries seemed to contrast with the relaxed, accepting style of those who supported Church and King - the Roundheads contrasted with the Cavaliers.

English forces at Waterloo

But crude generalisations from the battle lines of the 1640s do not explain much in the make-up of a nation of many millions. There are many other contrasts.

In the Middle Ages, the social structure rested on a broad base of land-working peasantry. Under the laws of the Anglo-Saxon kings and the "feudal system" of the Normans, most of these people were compelled to remain on the land of their lord. Landholdings throughout the country were recorded in the "Domesday Book" completed in 1086. Other social groups were far smaller. There were the townspeople, closely organised in guilds which controlled most aspects of their work; the clergy; tiny groups of transient specialised workers like master masons and stone carvers; a fringe population of beggars, lepers, criminals and outlaws. And, smallest group of all, the nobility.

The blasting effects of waves of disease like the Black Death of the late14th century and the recurrent plagues of the 16th, hindered any increase in population. At the time of the Norman Conquest England numbered around two million people. By the mid-14th century it was seven million, in Shakespeare's day perhaps under three million, but growing again. Real growth began in the 18th century. Massive growth and immigration in the 19th century brought it up from under 20 million to 40 million in the course of a hundred years, and transformed English life from a rural society with towns, into an urban society with a countryside.

This growth of population, the shift of emphasis from the land to the city, and the development of democracy, had a big impact on the social framework. Between the 15th and 17th centuries, increasing numbers and improved farming techniques may have stimulated each other, but there were periods of hunger and deprivation and

unrest when harvests failed, or when landowners "enclosed" land that villagers had previously shared. Local riots were common between the sixteenth and the nineteenth centuries; earlier there had been such uprisings as the Peasants' Revolt of 1381, when a rustic mob invaded London. But none of these pressures brought about a revolution.

In the face of protest, governments and landlords made - and sometimes later withdrew - concessions, rarely providing all that was asked, but taking the impetus out of unrest. The changes in population, the demands for manpower of an army and a merchant navy, the rise of industrial processes from the 13th century on, all meant that the social structure had to have some mobility and elasticity. England was a relatively small country, with good lines of communication. Public opinion had some power. Secure in their island, and with a distinct national spirit shared by all, the English allowed the fairly rigid social structure of the middle ages to evolve into the clearly defined but open class system of the 19th and 20th centuries. In this process, the rise of a social group unknown in the middle ages was vital. This was the middle class.

The nobility remained a tiny group at the social pinnacle, hardly

more numerous in the 18th century than in the 14th. At the base of the pyramid, the common people became ever more numerous. But the nature of social organisation was small local groups - villages with their squire and parson and cricket green, small towns with their mayors and aldermen. Each community had its own modest hierarchy. Linked by marriage and descent both to the lower levels of the aristocracy, and to the great mass of commoners, and spread throughout the country, the middle class became the great stabilising factor in society. The doctors, the lawyers, the better-off tenant farmers, the regular officers in army and navy, the clergymen, the factory-owners, the ship-owners, the bigger shopkeepers - as professions grew more various and more specialised, and required more education, so the middle class grew. Every town had its grammar school, enabling clever boys, a Shakespeare in the 16th century, a Samuel Johnson in the 18th (compiler of the first English dictionary), to achieve the learning that would enable brilliant careers.

The existence of the middle class had a great impact on cultural life. It was hungry for information, and many newspapers were started up from the 1780s on. It had leisure to read, and the great era of the English novel began in the 18th century. It had money for clothes, and London fashions spread. It wanted domestic comfort and a whole string of industries grew up to provide improved household furnishings and equipment. Kept at home by war, it had an urge to travel, and the first organised excursion was laid on by Thomas Cook in 1841.

Each class was very distinct, but the edges were increasingly blurred, and there was great mobility. As the nation's wealth increased by foreign trade and domestic mining and manufacturing from the early 18th century onwards, the aristocracy turned out not to be an exclusive caste. Commoners who made fortunes in trade and industry found that their daughters were quite eligible to become the brides of earls and viscounts. The great aristocratic families still controlled much of the nation's wealth, but the portion was diminishing. Though political power ebbed away from them, prestige remained, and with it the illusion of power. Titles and honours were eagerly sought after by men who found that money alone did not command respect.

The working class came to recognise itself in the 19th century, when thousands of people might work in a single factory. Out of these close-packed communities came such varying pastimes as Association Football and pigeon-racing. It formed its own protective bodies. Strenuously opposed by the employers, the trades unions grew in numbers and support, until they became an established part of the national fabric. Their political wing, the Labour Party, grew in the space of 30 years to be a mass party and formed its first government in 1924. Many people of conservative views expected something like the Russian Revolution. Instead, the new government looked and behaved remarkably like the old one.

Manufacturing in the 19th Century

ENGLAND AND THE MODERN WORLD

By the mid-sixteenth century, England had lost her European possessions and had simply become part of an off-shore island. Three hundred years later her empire spanned the globe and her fleet kept the peace at sea.. (Of course, following the union of 1707, it was the British Empire, but no-one has yet suggested that the Scots, Welsh or Irish, although heavily involved in the development of the empire, would have founded it without England. But England would have done it on its own).

Sea power was the great key. From Tudor times the English had developed a small but versatile and highly seaworthy ship that could act both as a merchantman and a man of war. In such vessels they sailed everywhere, on routes known and unknown. Sir Francis Drake's Golden Hind, one of the first ships to sail round the world, would seem a tiny vessel to us. Of only 120 tons, she nevertheless carried eighteen guns. London and Bristol were England's main ports, but dozens of smaller towns round the coast provided seamen, like Whitby, home of Captain Cook, who explored Eastern Australia and claimed it for Britain in 1769. The little ships carried emigrants and their supplies to North America, and carried back tobacco. As trade developed between the colonies and England, the ships became larger. In the 18th century, the handsome and well-armed vessels of the East India Company maintained communication and trade with the East. Specialised warships were developed. The great "ships of the line", formed into an invincible fleet under a series of fighting admirals of whom Nelson was the most outstanding, were the government's most deadly weapon in the Napoleonic Wars. "I do not say the French will not come", said Admiral St. Vincent, in 1803, "I only say, they will not come by sea." Nelson's flagship, HMS Victory, is still preserved at Portsmouth.

The seamen found the lands that formed the empire. Ten thousand miles from London, they had the same firm belief in England's superiority as their fellows at home. Their ships were often floating hells of disease, discomfort and relentless discipline. One crew, of HMS Bounty, famously mutinied in 1789 and colonised the remote Pitcairn Island. But worldwide trade developed, in tobacco, sugar, tea - products of the New World and the ancient East. England became the great entrepot of Western Europe, the place of exchange for commodities, and the London financial and insurance market grew in pace with the rise in commerce. The merchants needed to borrow money to finance their voyages and purchases; and they needed to take out protection against losing everything through storm or shipwreck. The great insurance market of Lloyds began in a London coffee-house, in 1692; two years later the government supported the establishment of the Bank of England.

In the age of the steamship, the vast colonial lands helped to feed England's mushrooming population. Wool, wheat, beef and butter became basic imports. After long and furious debate, freedom of trade had been gained with the repeal of the "Corn Laws" in 1846. For a period in the 19th century, England gained the name of "the workshop of the world". Raw materials such as cotton, timber,

An early steam locomotive

rubber, minerals, arrived by sea and were transformed into the factory-produced articles that went back by sea to every country. From railway locomotives to pins and needles, from battleships to bottled beer, "made in England" was the slogan.

For a country which in the 1600s had exported mainly wool, raw unfinished cloth, and salt fish, it was a remarkable change. The "Industrial Revolution" was a much more long-drawn out process than the name suggests. All through the 18th century, invention and experiment brought about more efficient and large-scale industrial techniques. Among the most important was iron-smelting, which became much more efficient early in the century. A bigger supply of better-quality iron enabled many other industrial developments to go forward.

Queen Victoria

The same kind of searching for new methods was making drastic changes in agriculture. Crop rotation, use of fertiliser, better ways of growing and storing seed all helped to produce bigger yields. Cross-breeding of animals on a scientific basis produced bigger and meatier cows and pigs. Fields and farms began to get bigger, and to employ fewer people. But now the workshops could offer employment to the redundant and dispossessed farm-workers. As the factories grew in size and number, people moved to meet the demand for labour. New industry also needed better transport, to take goods in bulk. New roads were built, the turnpikes, with toll-houses to charge the users, so that the surfaces could be maintained. The inland industrial towns like Leeds and Sheffield linked themselves to the sea by canals. Civil engineering works were carried out on a scale never seen before in England. The Pennine hills, separating the industrial areas of East and West, were tunnelled. Great aqueducts, like Pont-y-Cysyllte in North Wales, carried the canals across the valleys.

The increasing number of steam engines created extra demand for coal, and the engines themselves made it possible to dig far deeper than man had ever gone before. Landowners, like the Marquess of Stafford, who had coal deposits under their rolling acres, became enormously wealthy. Whole new towns, like Birmingham, appeared. In a few decades it grew from a village to be far bigger than the old cities like Bristol, York or Norwich. Some old towns, like Manchester, changed from being country markets to great manufacturing cities. The growth of the cities was unplanned and disorderly. In a country that was used to doing things in the traditional way, this explosive growth was hard to control, and reforms of local government trailed far behind the pace of social

change. As a result the new towns very soon became insanitary slums, and diseases like cholera arose.

A form of steam engine had been devised as early as 1698. Coal wagons already ran on wooden rails then. Steam traction was just a matter of time (it came in 1803, but the first really effective steam locomotive was built by George Stephenson in Northumberland in 1814). The power of steam drove the pace of change ever faster in the early part of the 19th century. The first public railway service opened between Stockton and Darlington, in North-East England, in 1823. Thirty years later, there was hardly a place of any size that was not joined to the railway network. Companies risked bankruptcy in building lines that competed for the same traffic. The writer and social reformer John Ruskin commented bitterly on one new line in the beautiful Peak District, "Now every fool in Buxton can be in Bakewell in thirty minutes, and vice versa". The era of mass travel had arrived.

One invention led to another and to a dozen more as people improved on the basic model. There was a frenzy of activity, and not just in commerce and industry. From the 1790s to the 1850s, English poetry passed through a period of development as rich and revolutionary as it had in the 16th century. The Lyrical Ballads of Wordsworth and Coleridge in 1798 declared the existence of the "Romantic" movement in literature, and it was eagerly followed up in many other countries. (Perhaps for the last time in England, poets were seen as politically dangerous: government agents shadowed the young Coleridge and Wordsworth - who later in life was to become Poet Laureate). During the 19th century it was the novelists, like Dickens, however, who grappled most effectively with the immense changes affecting society.

In other spheres, with painstaking application of scientific method, English scientists and thinkers made major contributions. Sir Humphrey Davey's safety lamp helped to reduce the appalling number of deaths in coal mines. Michael Faraday set out the principle of the electric motor. Sir Henry Bessemer's converter made mass production of steel a reality. Sir Rowland Hill introduced the adhesive postage stamp. Joseph Lister introduced carbolic antiseptic in medicine and surgery. There were new discoveries and developments in geology, chemistry, statistics and many other areas of knowledge. In 1859, Charles Darwin caused intense excitement and some horror with his publication of *The Origin of Species*.

By the later 19th century, London was the world's most populous city, and the world's busiest port. Its buildings were so

London Underground (circa 1880s)

densely-packed, and its streets so clogged with traffic, that the only solution was to put railways into underground tunnels. The atmosphere in these smoke-filled tubes was indescribable (some doctors actually sent their patients down there, for the benefit of their lungs. Medical science still had some way to go). Electric traction began in 1890 and brought some respite. In the heart of this teeming metropolis, a German political refugee sat in the Reading Room of the British Museum, and considered the enormous economic and social changes going on in the world, and led by England. He came to the view that revolutionary change must happen. The mass of working people would rise up against the system of Capital that controlled their lives. Karl Marx's theories were to be applied in some countries, but never in England. He died in London, and is buried there, among people in whom he recognised with some bafflement "a lack of revolutionary ardour".

Other nations were undergoing the same sort of changes during this period. They too have their inventors and discoverers. No one country can take all the credit, or blame. But the modern world of technology, applied science, mass mobility, spectator sports and consumer goods was first hatched in England.

Roman invasion of Britain, 55 BC

KEY DATES IN ENGLISH HISTORY (TO 1900)

BC

55 First Roman invasion

AD

40 Romans claim conquest

43 Foundation of Roman London

122 Emperor Hadrian visits. Hadrian's Wall begun

436 Departure of Roman troops

449 Major invasions by Angles and Saxons

597 Landing of St Augustine in Kent

664 Synod of Whitby

926 Athelstan king of all England

1066 Norman conquest of England

1086 Completion of Domesday Book

1154 Henry II, first Plantagenet king

1167 First English university, at Oxford

1170 Murder of Thomas Beckett

1215 Signing of Magna Carta by king John

1295 First representative Parliament, called by Edward I

1337 Hundred Years' War with France begins

1341 Establishment of House of Commons

1349 The Black Death reaches England

1388 Chaucer's Canterbury Tales

1453 End of Hundred Years' War

1455 Civil war begins between York and Lancaster

1474 First book printed in England

1485 Henry VII becomes first Tudor king

1505 Merchant Adventurers of All England receive royal charter

1534 Church of England breaks from Rome

1536 Suppression of the monasteries begins

1546 English Navy Board established

1558 Calais, last English possession in France, won by the French

1564 First horse-drawn coaches in England. Birth of William Shakespeare.

1565 Tobacco introduced to England

1574 First public theatre in England

1588 Defeat of Spanish Armada

1603 James I becomes first Stuart king of England

1605 Gunpowder Plot

1611 Authorised version of the Bible published

1632 First coffee house in London

1642 Civil War begins

1649 King Charles I executed

1660 Death of Oliver Cromwell, restoration of monarchy
    under Charles II

1665 Newton's discovery of gravitational theory

1666 Great Fire of London

1688 "The Glorious Revolution", William of Orange brought
    in as king

1694 Establishment of the Bank of England

1707 Union of England and Scotland as United Kingdom

1711 Newcomen develops a successful steam engine

1713 Last person executed for witchcraft

1731 "Law French" abandoned for English

1745 Scottish Jacobite army invades England

1755 Johnson's Dictionary of the English Language

1775 American War of Independence begins

1779 First cast-iron bridge built, over the Severn

1783 American independence conceded

1785 Daily Universal Register published, later renamed The
     Times

1793 War begins between Britain and revolutionary France

1796 Jenner uses anti-smallpox inoculation

1798 Publication of Lyrical Ballads by Wordsworth and
     Coleridge

1801 Trevithick develops a steam road carriage

1803 Trevithick develops first successful steam railway
     engine

1805 French and Spanish fleets defeated in Battle of
     Trafalgar

1815 End of Napoleonic Wars, with Battle of Waterloo

1819 Peterloo Massacre in Manchester

1823 Stockton & Darlington Railway opened

1832 First Parliamentary Reform Act

1834 Abolition of slavery in England

1837 Dickens publishes Pickwick Papers and Oliver Twist

1851 First double-decker omnibus

1859 Darwin publishes *The Origin of Species*

1863 First underground railway, London

1870 Elementary Education Act: schooling for all children

1874 First Trades Union MPs elected

1884 First practical steam turbine developed by Parsons

1891 First Labour member of Parliament (Keir Hardie)

1895 London's first motor-car exhibition

1899 Wireless telegraphy begins from England to France

LARDIL

KEEPERS OF THE DREAMTIME

DAVID MCKNIGHT

TRIBAL WISDOM

CHRONICLE BOOKS

SAN FRANCISCO

A Labyrinth Book

First published in the United States in 1995 by Chronicle Books.

Design by Generation Associates

The Little Wisdom Library —Tribal Wisdom was produced by Labyrinth Publishing Ltd.

Printed and bound in Italy by L.E.G.O.

Library of Congress Cataloging in Publication Data: McKnight, David. The Lardil of aboriginal Australia : keepers of the dreamtime / by David McKnight. p . cm.

ISBN 0–8118–0834–3

1. Lardil (Australian people)—History. 2. Mythology, Lardil.
3. Lardil (Australian people)—Rites and ceremonies.   1. Title
DU125.L37M35 1995
306.4'0994—dc20   94-40058
                                                                          CIP

Distributed in Canada by Raincoast Books,
8680 Cambie Street Vancouver, B.C. V6P 6M9
10 9 8 7 6 5 4 3 2 1

Chronicle Books

275 Fifth Street, San Francisco, CA 94103

Introduction

Above: Children are familiar with their environment from an early age and soon become accomplished hunters. *Previous pages:* Lardil elders performing a corroboree. This dance is about the suffering of the Rainbow Serpent.

uropean settlement in Australia occurred in 1788 with the arrival of the First Fleet in the area of Sydney harbor. At that time the population of Aboriginal Australia was no less than 300,000, and it was probably much more. It dropped to less than 100,000 at the turn of this century, but since then the aboriginal population has noticeably increased. The tribes in the vicinity of Sydney harbor were soon decimated by diseases, ecological disturbances and harsh treatment. These events were to be repeated again and again wherever European settlements were established. In later years the Aborigines were forced into reserves, government settlements, and missions. The reasons for this are complex, but much rests on the fact that the economies and uses of the land by Europeans and Aborigines were diametrically opposed. The European settlers were agriculturists and pastoralists, while the Australian Aborigines were hunters and gatherers. The settlers justified their acquisition of the land on the grounds that the Aborigines did not use or occupy the land and that Australia was *terra nullius,* no one's land.

Page 4: Burrurr ("Seaweed") is an outstanding craftsman, as can be seen by his shield and dancing hat.
Page 7: "Morning Glory," a unique natural phenomenon that occurs in the Gulf of Carpentaria. One huge cloud comes sweeping over the horizon at the end of winter.

This view held sway for over two hundred years until it was successfully challenged in the Australian High Court in 1992, when it was ruled that native title had not necessarily been extinguished.

Underlying the Aborigines' firm economic tie with their land is a powerful religious bond. Much of their religious thinking is based on the beliefs of the Dreamtime and the totemic or ancestral heroes. These beliefs vary from tribe to tribe but there is a common thread. For the Aborigines, the Dreamtime is everlasting and unchangeable and thus contrasts with the everyday world which is subject to extreme changes. The Dreamtime is a period that took place before the appearance of human beings. People identify with the totemic beings of the Dream-time, and they are often regarded as the reincarnation of these beings.

Opposite: The rocky points of south Mornington Island often form boundaries between Aboriginal countries. *Following pages:* Sandy beaches with she oaks are characteristic features of much of the northern area of Mornington Island. People camp under she oaks, and it is taboo to cut them because this might induce a storm.

$$=$$

The Wellesley
Islands

$$=$$

The people of the Wellesley Islands, in the Gulf of Carpentaria in Northern Queensland, had little contact with white Australians until this century. The Wellesley Islands are the territories of three tribes, the Kaiadilt of Bentinck Island, the Yangkaal of the Forsyth Islands (including Denham Island), and the Lardil of Mornington Island. Each tribe has had a different history of first contact. The Kaiadilt was the last group of Aborigines in this region to come under white dominance. In the late 1940s, having suffered severely from a shortage of food and internal conflict, they volunteered to emigrate to Mornington Island. The Yangkaal were disrupted through the establish-

Above: A Lardil fisherman proudly displays his catch for the day.

ment of Burketown (a port settlement) on the banks of the Albert River. Burketown drew them and neighboring mainland tribes as if it were a social magnet. The Aborigines were interested to see the strange sights and to acquire tea, sugar, tobacco, knives, and axes.

Lardil contact with white Australians began in 1915 when a Presbyterian Mission was founded on Mornington Island. Aborigines from the mainland were forcibly sent to the mission by the police and the Protector of the Aborigines. The children were separated from their parents and placed in dormitories—one for girls and another for boys. The mission hegemony continued until the early 1970s

when Mornington Island and the surrounding region became a Shire and so came under the political control of the Queensland government.

Above: A sea turtle, whose flesh is highly prized among the Lardil.

The Wellesley Island Aborigines were fortunate in that they have continued to reside in their tribal territories which were never effectively taken away from them. Nevertheless for many years they suffered disruption; their freedom to act according to their own laws and follow their own religious practices was subject to outside control. Nowadays the crucial dilemma for the people is how to live a life that accords their own traditions with the restraints as well as the opportunities that have been introduced by outsiders. This problem is one which is common throughout Aboriginal Australia. Many Aborigines have sought a solution through the Homeland Movement which involves a return to their clan lands, where they can follow their traditional practices.

Lardil tribal territory covers an area of approximately 400 square miles and is divided into over thirty countries. The sizes of the countries vary but none of them is very large. One result of the small size of the countries is that members must interact with their neighbors. Each country consists of an area along the shore as well as inland bush. Hence the members have access to both seafood and land food. Each country is identified with a group of people who regard themselves

Opposite: Children are encouraged to participate in dances and are decorated with white clay.

as being patrilineally related—deriving descent through the father. For example, a country may consist of three brothers and two sisters who have the same father. They may have different mothers but that does not affect their claims to the country. The children of the three brothers are members of the country. But the children of the two sisters belong to the country of their husbands. Countries are known by their main camping places or by the name of the eldest member. Lardil personal names are drawn from the natural world, particularly the sea. Members of a country have special economic, residential, and spiritual rights. Most important are their rights to prized portions of dugong (sea cows) and sea turtle. People feel secure in their own country for they know where both the mystically safe and dangerous places are. In their own country they can do as they please, hunt and gather as they wish, cut a branch from a tree to make a digging stick or a spear, and they can camp in any location of their choice for as long as they want. In short, they are free from outside restraint.

Opposite: Body decoration. Red ochre is often used to paint representations of lightning.

People of the Sea

Opposite: The right to the sea gives the Lardil rights to the dugong (sea cow), which is one of their culinary delicacies. *Above:* Man on a stone fish trap. Fish are left stranded in these as the tide recedes. *Previous pages:* A Lardil elder enacting a ritual to induce a storm in order to punish his enemies.

The Wellesley Islands are a particularly rich hunting and gathering area. The islanders have long viewed themselves as people of the sea and located their main camps (as they still do) near the beach so that they had an unobstructed view of the sea. From the sea they obtained fish, shellfish, crabs, turtles, and dugong. The area is a breeding ground for sea turtle and dugong, which are highly prized game and play a major part in the people's diet. The traditional methods of hunting these large sea creatures involved nets and spears. Nowadays outboard motors and harpoons are used.

The Lardil occasionally trapped sea turtles and dugong in the two major rivers, Sandalwood River and Dugong River. At low tide a line of bushes was extended from both banks. Large nets were placed in the middle and held by two or more hunters. As a school of dugong went up the river at high tide in search of rich grass, other hunters got behind them on rafts to cut off their line of retreat. The dugong rushed forward in a panic and became entangled in the nets. The hunt was considered dangerous for the men holding the nets because they ran the risk of also being entangled and suffering broken limbs.

The large sea turtles, which often weigh over two hundred pounds, crawl up the sandy beaches to dig nests for their eggs. Although it is easy to discover the whereabouts of a nest it is not always easy for a hunter to find the exact location of the eggs. A hunter breaks off a stick from a tree (or he may use his spear) and pokes it in the sand where he thinks that the eggs may be. He keeps doing this until the stick goes easily into the sand and he then starts digging. But this is easier said than done because when the sand is very loose, it is difficult to discern the difference between one place and another. The hunter may not have dug in the exact location and as a result he is likely to heap sand over the place where the eggs in fact are. In this case the site becomes so disturbed that an unskillful hunter is unable to find the eggs. A more knowledgeable hunter may come after him and realize what has happened from the many footprints and holes and prove to be more skillful.

Around the evening fire, people enjoy talking about their hunting and gathering exploits and recounting the day's events. In this way, younger people learn about where the best places are for hunting, the habits of fish and animals, and how to track.

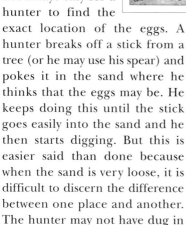

For instance, one man tells the story of how he became an accomplished hunter. As a youth, whenever he threw his spear and missed a fish his father would strike him on the arm with his spear thrower. Children are encouraged to hunt and when they are successful they are highly praised. It does not matter that they may have only caught a small fish or a small lizard. The Lardil regard it as very bad manners to criticize someone's efforts, because this creates ill feeling, and the person criticized may decide to take revenge. When it comes to cooked food, the receiver should never complain that it is undercooked or overcooked. No matter how raw or burnt it may be, one should eat it without complaint. To complain is to dishonor the food and the giver. It dishonors the food because in its natural state it was clean and pure, and people do not have the right to complain about animals in their natural state; it dishonors the giver because he or she has given food out of generosity, and one has no right to complain about a person's generous action.

Above: A hunting expedition culminates in the successful capture of a sea turtle.
Opposite: Searching for turtle's eggs buried in the sand on the beach.

The Dreamtime

Australian Aborigines lead a spiritual existence, where land and society are seen as mutually dependent. The Aborigine acknowledges the demands of the world, but these are not in conflict with spiritual expression. In fact all the elements of this "cosmic drama" are interrelated. The land possesses the Aborigine, just as the land is possessed by the Aborigine.

Australian Aborigines are well-known for their deep spiritual attachment to their land and their beliefs about totemic Ancestral Beings. Our understanding of Aboriginal Australia and why the Aborigines struggled so fiercely against being dispossessed of their land depends on our grasp of these two key values. For Australians of European descent, land is important as an economic resource. The economic nature of land is well recognized by the Aborigines because for them land is both their father and mother; it nurtures them and provides shelter.

Above: Lardil dancers decorate their bodies with bird down to represent Dreamtime beings. *Opposite:* Shell middens are occasionally found on high ground near mangroves. Their occurrence is evidence of frequent use of the site. *Previous pages:* An Aboriginal bark painting by the Queensland artist Mandarrk (1979).

But land is much more than an economic good. It is a mystical phenomenon which forms the heart of Aboriginal religious beliefs and practices. Many of their sacred stories pertain to the land. To travel in their countries is a religious experience because the landscape pulsates with power left by the Dreamtime beings as they performed their wondrous deeds.

The Dreamtime is at the very core of the Aborigine's belief system. This is the time of the ancestor, the mythical period when the totemic Ancestral Beings appeared and began to transform the world. The Dreamtime is transmitted through oral traditions and paintings, and it recounts their wanderings across immense territories, modifying the landscape, creating flora, fauna, and humankind, and teaching the people their ceremonies.

The creative acts of the Ancestral Beings are sacred to each Aboriginal tribe and form the basis and justification for the entire religious life of the tribe. The Dreamtime came to an end when the Ancestral Beings left the surface of the earth, but their departure did not signify the loss of this mythical past, for it can be periodically recovered through ritual. Slowly, through initiation rites and other ceremonies, the sacred myths of the Dreamtime that reveal the meaning of their lives are unfolded. Thus the Dreamtime is not a static mythical period. It is once again present through the reenactment of certain rituals and customs.

It is the duty of Aborigines to reenact the events of the Dreamtime beings in rituals and ceremonies. When they perform the rituals they become the Dreamtime beings and are able to tap into the power of the land and these Ancestral Beings. This power can be dangerous. Those who know their country are safe from unwittingly breaking taboos,

Above: The dancer's totemic dreaming is Fire, and in this instance he has used charcoal for his body design.

but unknowledgeable strangers may, in their ignorance, blunder into sacred story places which may, in turn, unleash meteorological forces or cause them to become ill and to die. Hence in Aboriginal Australia people fear to visit strange and unknown places unaccompanied by an owner or holder of the land. It is small wonder that wars of conquest over land between tribes have rarely, if ever, occurred.

In all tribes there are songs and myths about land. Song men and song women praise the abundance and beauty of their countries and they chant the names of the various places, the location of water holes, swamps, and rich food places. In their songs they recount the journeys of the cultural heroes and the sacred story sites. It is by such means that young people become familiar with all aspects of their country. By these songs the singers not only express their emotional attachment to their land, but also they give voice to their claims to the land. It is their right to sing the songs, to relate the myths, and to perform the sacred dances. Other people may do so only if they are invited to participate. To break these laws is to risk an attack by the elders and men of mystical powers. Hence the land not only protects itself but it is protected by its people.

Opposite: A Lardil elder adorns himself with body paint.

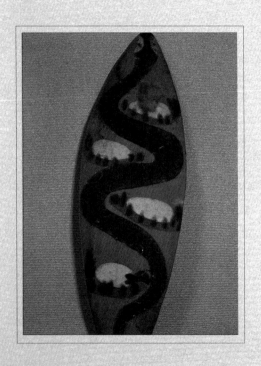

The

Rainbow

Serpent

A deeper understanding of the Lardil society can be obtained by examining what they refer to as *yuuringman ngalu*, myths or sacred stories of long ago. A particularly important myth is that of the Rainbow Serpent. The events of the myth are believed to have occurred when the Wellesley Islands were joined to the mainland. The time of year of the myth is at the end of the dry season when the rainy season is expected to begin.

Rainbow Serpent—*Thuwathu*—builds a rainproof shelter at the mouth of the Dugong River in anticipation of the torrential rain. The Dugong River is known as *Minyindagarr*—suffering man—for reasons which the myth makes

Above: An unusually large wooden artefact of the Rainbow Serpent in his shelter. The colors red and white are often used to symbolize blood and sea foam. *Previous pages:* A painting of the Rainbow Serpent, which also represents Dugong River, which he created.

Above: A wind dance. In the foreground one dancer plays the didgeridoo (a wooden wind instrument) while in the background, another dancer holds a boomerang which represents a rib of the Rainbow Serpent.

clear. Soon the rain falls and his sister pleads with him to give shelter to her baby daughter, his niece. But he claims that there is not enough room because he needs it for his two heads. She returns when the rain is heavier and pleads for shelter, but again he claims that he needs it for his two arms. Still later she returns and pleads for shelter for her daughter, but he still refuses because he needs the room for his two legs. And so the story continues, with Rainbow Serpent's sister pleading for shelter for her baby and each time Rainbow Serpent refusing on the pretence that there is only enough space for himself. His claims are false because each time his sister sees space in his shelter he purposely moves over to occupy it.

Eventually the baby dies of cold and exposure, and in revenge Rainbow Serpent's sister sets fire to his shelter. In his agony Rainbow Serpent swirls around and around and finally bursts out of the shelter in an attempt to escape the flames. In his suffering he makes Dugong River, where the stones are said to be his blood, reefs his back bone, and messmate trees his ribs. The power of boomerangs are said to derive from the fact that they are made from messmate trees, and are therefore Rainbow Serpent's ribs. Eventually Rainbow Serpent reaches a spring and when the people see him suffering they cut their arms and legs with shells just as the Lardil do to this day when their relatives are dying. Rainbow Serpent went down the spring and died. One obvious message of this myth is that failure to share one's resources may end in death.

Often when the Lardil see a rainbow they draw attention to the colors, particularly the red, and in a sad tone they recall how Rainbow Serpent suffered from burns. Rainbows are regarded as a reflection of the Rainbow Serpent, who is believed to be lurking in the sea. And as a rainbow is a reflection from below to above this means that the top of a rainbow is the under part of Rainbow Serpent, and the under part of a rainbow is the top part of the Rainbow Serpent. Rainbow

Above: This stone is from the Dingo Story site. Most story places are dangerous to outsiders, particularly if they break the taboo of mixing land food with seafood.

Serpent is said not to like rain and that he eats it up. As we know, a rainbow appears in the sky after a storm and hence it is a sign that the rain is finished.

The Rainbow Serpent is believed to be a force for good and evil. Medicine men are said to obtain their powers for healing by capturing a small rainbow at a water hole. Sorcerers also gain power from the Rainbow Serpent and their powers are much feared, particularly by people from outside their country. The Rainbow Serpent is identified with a sickness known as *marlkirii* (*marl* meaning hand; *kirii* meaning to wash). This sickness occurs primarily when people mix land food and seafood outside their own country. Each country is protected by a *marlkirii* being. This

being is said to know the scent of the members of a country. But when a stranger appears, the *marlkirii* being senses danger. If a stranger mixes food from the two

Above: A Lardil artist weaving a dance artefact from human hair.

environments then the *marlkirii* being attacks. Whenever people move from the sea to the land or vice versa, care should be taken to eliminate the traces and smell of grease, fat, and blood. Hence a man coming out of the sea after hunting for fish, sea turtle, and dugong should wash his hands and mouth with fresh water. He should at least purify his hands by rubbing them with sand. If he then goes inland to, say, a water lily swamp, then he should water his hands with mud from the edges of the swamp. The beach area, which is not quite land and not quite sea, is a neutral area which is by and large free from the danger of *marlkirii* sickness.

Each *marlkirii* being is a local manifestation of the Rainbow Serpent; each is the Rainbow Serpent under a different guise. When a person is sickened with *marlkirii* he can be cured by an owner of the country who knows the *marlkirii* song. Essentially this song recalls Rainbow Serpent's suffering and in the song the parts of his body are sung in the same order that Rainbow Serpent in the myth listed them as an excuse for not sheltering his baby niece. The person suffering from *marlkirii* sickness normally has a painful swollen abdomen accompanied by a rash and a headache. The singer presses the stricken person's abdomen, rubs his scent on him, and ties a string made of human hair to his foot and places the other end into the sea. While he is doing this he chants the *marlkirii* song. People know that the sufferer has been healed when they see a shooting star. A red or green shooting star is believed to be the eye of the Rainbow Serpent. It is taboo to point at a colored shooting star or to draw attention to it because someone may become ill from a sorcerer or the Rainbow Serpent. A white shooting star is not considered to be dangerous. It is a sign that one will find (that is conceive or beget) a baby or that one will find sea turtle eggs.

Above: A Lardil man plays a didgeridoo, and grasps a boomerang in his other hand.

The Life Cycle

child spirit indicates a desire to come into the human world by giving his or her parents-to-be a sign which is usually something out of the ordinary. A man for example may have harpooned a young dugong by a single thrust while other hunters continually miss. This is taken as a sign that the hunter and his wife have found or are going to find a baby. The child's conception sign is young dugong and the child may be given special rights to that kind of dugong in the region where the conception sign occurred. Many people draw attention to birth marks and physical peculiarities as evidence as to what occurred to them in Dreamtime and as proof that such a happening was their conception sign. A new-born baby is nameless until people are assured that it is

Above: Traditionally the Lardil had several types of shelter. The above is one of the simplest: nevertheless it gives excellent protection from the cold southeast wind. *Previous pages:* Waterlily swamps are highly valued as a source of food. The lilies may only be picked when the senior member of the country gives permission.

going to stay with them. When they are convinced that the child is here to stay he or she is given a name by a grandparent or an older distantly related brother or sister. They often give their own name so as to stress the relationship and their common identity. The male's dominant role in procreation is reflected in the belief that a child looks and walks like his or her father, and above all that a child has the same shaped foot as the

Above: Hair belts are made from human hair, and they should only be worn by initiated men.

father. So familiar are the Lardil with people's tracks that they are easily able to determine a person's identity from his or her footprint and how long ago a track was made.

When a child is about five years old a *yirri* (umbilical cord) ceremony is held. The child's maternal relatives heap nets, spears, boomerangs, digging sticks, and hairbelts in front of the child. On top of the heap is the umbilical cord which is wrapped in bark. From birth, this cord is taken care of by the mother and her father and siblings. The ceremony indicates the authority and responsibility of the maternal relatives. Later in life, male youths go through two initiation rituals: the first is *luruku*—circumcision—and the second is *warama*—subincision. During these two rituals a youth is taught tribal law, particularly how one's sister and sister's child should be treated. After the first initiation he is forbidden to speak Lardil for over a year. He must communicate by sign language. In the second initiation he is taught a complex language known as *Demiin*. This language has click consonants and is unique in Aboriginal Australia. Both these languages classify the world in a different way from Lardil language and hence present different world views.

As is the case throughout Aboriginal Australia, the Lardil, the Yangkaal, and the Kaiadilt have complex marriage laws. A man is expected to marry his second cousin—the

Above: A young man preparing himself for a ceremony by painting his body.

daughter of his mother's mother's brother's daughter. This may seem very difficult to understand, and to a certain extent it is, but the underlying principle is simply that the children of two female cross-cousins or two male cross-cousins should marry. As one Lardil woman put it: "What we find we share with our cousins, even our children. These are the only correct marriages for all other marriages are considered irregular." In the past, a proposed irregular marriage evoked such fierce opposition that the young couple involved would elope to the mainland in order to escape being speared.

The camp fire is one center of family life. And normally only a married couple and their children

Above: Lardil children at an outstation camp.

shared the same camp fire. As brothers matured and had their own families, so they had separate fireplaces. Similarly each family had their own bark shelter or windbreak. The bark shelters were so well made that they were waterproof against the torrential rains of the monsoons.

As is the case with fireplaces, brothers shared the same shelter with their parents, but when they matured they had their own shelter. Because of the incest taboo that existed and was strongly enforced among the Lardil, brother and sister were forbidden to share the same fireplace and shelter.

At death the life cycle is completed as the deceased's spirit returns to Dreamtime. The name of a recently dead person may not be said, just as initially there is no name for a new-born child. To mention the name of a dead person is to risk the wrath of the deceased's close relatives, because saying the deceased's name reminds them of their bereavement. The dead are usually referred to in a roundabout way and often by the place where death occurred. Just as an unborn child is identified with the place where his or her coming into being was indicated by a sign, so the dead are known by the place where they went out of being.

Above: An abstract representation of three ancestral beings who created many sites in the Wellesley Islands.

Death is not to be feared for there is no heaven or hell. At death people return to where they came from. Life is thus a transition from coming into being, from Dreamtime *(karnannunnge)*, to going out of being, to Dreamtime. For the Lardil this living world is only a shadow of the reality of Dreamtime.

In their world view, the Lardil see themselves as belonging to the natural world just like other creatures. They believe that in Dreamtime they and the animals were one. But because of a split in time, the world we live in became partially separated from the dream world, and as a result human beings became separated from other animals. Human beings learned to make fire, to speak language, to follow the incest taboo, and to have kin. Although this differentiates humans from animals, it does not make humans better than animals.

Above: Nowadays, Aboriginal art is highly sought after. Here, Goobalathaldin, a famous Lardil artist, paints a bark painting.

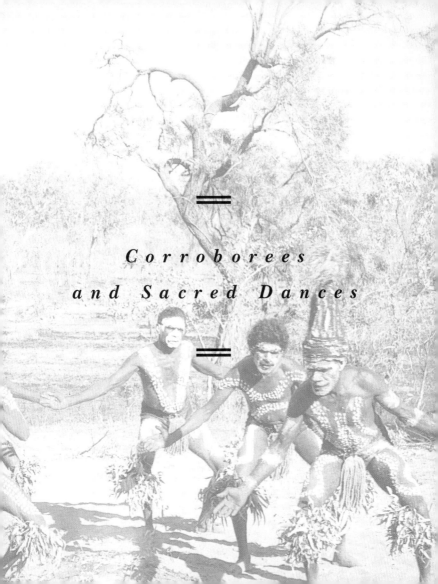

Corroborees

and Sacred Dances

I t is in dances and special ceremonies called corroborees that much of the religious beliefs and practices about Dreamtime is given expression. The Lardil believe that in their dreams they are able to slip into Dreamtime. In dreams the fantastic occurs and the Dreamtime beings sing and show themselves as they really are. A dreamer who has slipped into Dreamtime sings in his sleep, though the Lardil believe that it is not really the dreamer who is singing, but the Dreamtime beings through the dreamer. From what the dreamer sees in his dream a dance is made up. Anyone who was at the camp when the dream occurred has a right to participate in the dance.

Left: The decoration of this dancer represents Top Knot Pigeon, which is the main totemic dreaming of his country. *Previous pages:* This corroboree enacts the suffering of the Rainbow Serpent caused by the burning of his shelter. Note the ashes in the background.

Dancers decorate themselves with white clay, red ochre, and bird down. Black, which is obtained from charcoal, is rarely used and normally connotes emptiness such as a reef hole or the empty space contained in the Milky Way. These body designs are representations of the totemic beings with which the dancers are identified. The body designs may be Sea, Flying Fox, Stingray, Lightning, Dog, or others. The dancers wear two types of hat which are made out of bark and human hair. A cone-shaped hat is normally worn by dancers who identify with the Rainbow Serpent and the Sea; a crown-shaped hat is worn by men who identify with Lightning and Dog. In making body designs, bird down is rolled into small balls which formerly were stuck on the body by using blood drawn from the forearm (now any adhesive is used). In addition to hats, initiation men have the right to wear human hair belts and a finely woven headband made out of fiber string. Normally, teeth are attached to the sides of the headband. These are wallaby teeth, but they represent dog teeth.

Above: This Lardil elder performs a corroboree. The white marking on his dancing hat represents a column of smoke as well as clouds.

Dog teeth are not used because they are considered to be too powerful. The Lardil believe that in Dreamtime, Man and Dog both went through the first initiation, but in the second initiation Dog took fright and ran away while Man bravely endured the pain. In this way the Lardil explain the differences and similarities between dogs and human beings.

Because of their contact with non-Aboriginal people, the Wellesley Islanders have had to cope with many changes in their marriage laws, child-rearing practices, education, camp life, and religious practices. One of the problems that the new types of European houses created for them is that they do not allow the subtle expression of the

social distinctions that is so important in the traditional social organization. Brothers and sisters, for instance, share the same room or at least are now obliged to live in the same house. In the past they had separate shelters and they avoided one another. The expense of maintaining houses and the division of household roles causes problems and in some cases the houses have been abandoned. One of the reasons for the recent return to clan lands, what is popularly known as the Outstation Movement or the Homeland Movement, is to escape the stress of the larger settlements and the European style of housing.

The missionaries prevented the men from having more than one wife and this changed not only the marriage practices but also family life and kin relationships. For many years initiation ceremonies were prohibited and as a result many young men were not taught the sacred laws or the initiation languages. When the power of the Mission waned, initiation ceremonies were revived with the help of ritual leaders from the mainland. In these and other matters, the Wellesley Islanders have asserted their right to self determination. They and other Aborigines are now vigorously fighting for their land rights and they are struggling to protect their land from the encroachment of mining corporations

Above: This is one of the first Lardil efforts to construct a house at an outstation.
Notice the Aboriginal flag and the ant bed oven.

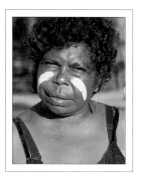

Elder, Bruce. *Blood on the Wattle.*
Australia: National Book
Distributors, 1992.

McKnight, David. "Fighting in an
Australian Aboriginal
Supercamp." In David Riches
(ed.), *The Anthropology of Violence.*
Oxford: Basil Blackwell, 1986.

Reynolds, Henry. *The Law of the
Land.* London: Penguin Books,
1992.

Roughsey, Dick. *Moon and
Rainbow: The Autobiography of an
Aboriginal.* Australia: Rigby
International, 1977.

Trezise, Percy. *Dream Road.*
Australia: Allen & Unwin, 1993.

Bell, Diane. *Daughters of the Dreaming*. Australia: Allen & Unwin, 1993.

Keen, Ian. *Knowledge and Secrecy in an Aboriginal Religion*. Oxford: Clarendon Press, 1994.

Maddock, Kenneth. *The Australian Aborigines*, Australia: Penguin Books, 1982.

Morphy, Howard. *Ancestral Connections*. Chicago: University of Chicago Press, 1991.

Myers, Fred. *Pintupi Country, Pintupi Self*. Washington: Smithsonian Institution; Canberra: Australian Institute of Aboriginal Studies,1986.

Ross, Helen. *Just for Living: Aboriginal Perceptions of Housing in Northwest Australia*. Canberra: Australian Institute of Aboriginal Studies, 1987.

Swain, Tony. *A Place for Strangers*. Australia: Cambridge University Press, 1993.

Every effort has been made to trace all present copyright holders of the material used in this book, whether companies or individuals. Any omission is unintentional, and we will be pleased to correct errors in future editions of this book.

Text Acknowledgments:

When I first started my research among the Mornington Islanders in 1966 there were elders who had once lived at a time when there were no white people on Mornington Island. The elders were very interested in my work and they went out of their way to teach me about Lardil customs and the traditional way of life. I would like to take this opportunity to express my deep gratitude to them and to all the people of Mornington Island who helped me in so many ways.

Picture Acknowledgments:

Axel Poignant: Page 17.
Bridgeman Art: Page 28.

All other images are the property of David McKnight.